THE PENGUIN POETS

FRAGMENTS FROM THE FIRE

Chris Llewellyn was born and raised in Fostoria, Ohio. She
studied writing with Marilyn Hacker at The George Washington
University, where she also took a degree in political science,
and has been a Poet in Residence at the Festival of Poets
and Poetry at St. Mary's College in Maryland. Her poems have
appeared in many journals and anthologies, and she has read
in the United States Congress, at the Folger Shakespeare Library,
and elsewhere. Llewellyn identifies herself primarily as
a "labor poet," and is married to Edward Bordley, who has
translated her poems into Spanish. They live in Washington, D.C.

Winner of the

WALT WHITMAN AWARD for 1986

Sponsored by the Academy of American Poets,
the Walt Whitman Award is given annually
to the winner of an open competition among American poets
who have not yet published their first books of poetry.

Judge for 1986: Maxine Kumin

# FRAGMENTS FROM THE FIRE

## The Triangle Shirtwaist Company Fire of March 25, 1911

*P O E M S  B Y*

### Chris Llewellyn

*PENGUIN
BOOKS*

gift
Dr. mdS

PENGUIN BOOKS
Viking Penguin Inc., 40 West 23rd Street,
New York, New York 10010, U.S.A.
Penguin Books Ltd, Harmondsworth,
Middlesex, England
Penguin Books Australia Ltd, Ringwood,
Victoria, Australia
Penguin Books Canada Limited, 2801 John Street,
Markham, Ontario, Canada L3R 1B4
Penguin Books (N.Z.) Ltd, 182–190 Wairau Road,
Auckland 10, New Zealand

First published in 1987 in simultaneous hardcover
and paperback editions by Viking Penguin Inc.
Published simultaneously in Canada

"The Great Divide" and "Ninth Floor Reprise" first appeared in *Building Blocks*,
National Center for Urban Ethnic Affairs; "March 25, 1911" in *The Washington Review*;
"Twenty-sixth Street Pier," "At Rest in Greenwood" and "Potter's Field" in *Quindaro*;
"Funeral for the Nameless" in *The Chester H. Jones Foundation National Poetry Competition
Winners 1983*; "White Light" in *Talkin' Union*; "Stitcher" in *13th Moon*; "Sear" in *Evidence
of Community*, Center for Washington Area Studies; and "Triangle Site" in *Working Cultures*.

Photographs on pages 15, 33, 39, 57, and 65 are courtesy of the Library of Congress
Photograph on page 23 is courtesy of Brown Brothers
Photograph on page 45 is courtesy of Florence Leebov

LIBRARY OF CONGRESS CATALOGING IN PUBLICATION DATA
Llewellyn, Chris.
Fragments from the fire.
Bibliography: p.
1. Triangle Shirtwaist Company—Fire, 1911—
Poetry.   I. Title.
[PS3562.L67F7   1987b]       811'.54       86-16932
ISBN 0 14 058.586 9

Printed in the United States of America by
R. R. Donnelley & Sons Company, Harrisonburg, Virginia
Set in Memphis Medium and Souvenir Light Italic

Poems concerning the Triangle Fire
of March 25, 1911, are written
in memory of sisters who died in the Fire—
Bettina and Frances Miale,
Rosalie and Lucia Maltese,
Sara and Sarafine Sariciano—
and are dedicated to my sisters,
Sara Jane Reinhart and Elizabeth Ann James.

## Acknowledgments

The author wishes to thank the District of Columbia
Arts and Humanities Commission for a 1984 grant which
funded technical assistance for the manuscript.

Also thanks to those critical readers of the manuscript:
Anne Becker, Kamal Boullata, Deborah George, Judith Hall,
Elizabeth Ann James, Michael Kernan, Mary Ann Larkin,
Carrie McKee, Jean Nordhaus, and Saul Schniderman.

The author acknowledges the continued support
of the Capitol Hill Poetry Group, the Jennie McKean Moore
Writing Program, and the Festival of Poets and Poetry
at St. Mary's College of Maryland.

## AUTHOR'S NOTE

The Triangle Shirtwaist Company manufactured blouses
for women and was located on the eighth, ninth, and tenth floors
of the Asch Building, at the corner of Washington Place
and Greene Street, in New York City's Washington Square.
The company employed up to 900 workers at a time,
but on March 25, 1911, only about 500 were present.
These were immigrants, most of whom could not speak
the English language. Nearly all were female, primarily Russian
or Italian, although twelve nationalities were known to be
"on the books."

At about 4:45 p.m., just after pay envelopes had been
distributed, a fire broke out. Not everyone was able to reach
the elevators and stairways. On the ninth floor, because the
bosses had kept the doors locked to keep out union organizers,
workers were forced to jump from windows. One hundred forty-
six people, some as young as fourteen, perished.

# CONTENTS

To proclaim the acceptable year of the Lord;
to appoint unto them that mourn in Zion,
to give unto them beauty for ashes . . .
the garment of praise for the spirit
of heaviness.

—*Isaiah 61:2, 3*

# THE GREAT DIVIDE

Henry Street, Cherry Street, Hester Street:
the new world turns toward old Jerusalem.
Sunrays stream on the bearded father-singers
standing beside a hundred rag-stuffed windows.

Chant the "Havdallah," chant "The Great Divide."

They praise the Almighty for creating us a Sabbath
that cuts one day away from the fabric of the week.
Bent over Singers, their backs to factory windows,
women and children stitch into sunset.

Wait for the darkness, time for going home.

They piecework shirtwaists under the company sign—
the letters set in English, Hebrew, Italian:
"If you don't show up on Saturday or Sunday,
you've already been fired when it's Monday."

Chant the "Havdallah," chant "The Great Divide."

Still the sun drops, and the fathers pour
the ritual wine into a little platter.
Each strikes a sulphur-tip match, touches
the surface of the small wine lake.

Light in the windows, dividing up the dark.

# MARCH 25, 1911

It was Spring. It was Saturday.
Payday. For some it was Sabbath.
Soon it will be Easter. It was
approaching April, nearing Passover.
It was close to closing time.

The heads of trees budding
in Washington Square Park.
The sun a hot flywheel spinning
the earth's axle. The days long
enough for leaving in light.
           It was Spring.

America's sweethearts—the ladies—
stroll in shirtwaists of lawn and lace,
mimic Charles Dana Gibson's Girls.
They pose in finery cut from bolts of
flimsy and stitched by garment girls
on Gibbs, Wilcox, and Singer machines.
           It was Saturday.

Up in the Asch Building
in the Triangle Shirtwaist Company
Rosie Glantz is singing "Every Little
Movement Has a Meaning of Its Own."
Fixing hair, arranging puffs and tendrils,
the other girls in the cloakroom join in:
"Let me call you Sweetheart,
I'm in love with you."
           It was Payday.

Attar-of-roses, lily of the valley,
still they smell of machine oil
that soaks the motors and floors.

The barrel in each stairwell
could fill a thousand lamps.
                        For some it was Sabbath.

Here at Triangle, Sophie Salemi
and Della Costello sew on Singers.
Neighbors from Cherry Street,
they piecework facing each other,
the oil pan hitting their knees.
Tomorrow sisters will nail flowers
on tenement doors.
                        Soon it will be Easter.

The machine heads connected by belts
to the flywheel to rotating axle
sing the Tarantella. Faster,
faster vibrate the needles, humming
faster the fashionable dance.
                        It was approaching April.

Della and Sophie up on Ninth
piece sleeves, race the needle's pace
not knowing on Eighth, paper patterns
burn from the wire, fall on machines,
spark moths and pinwheels round the room.
Rockets push up cutting-tables.
                        It was nearing Passover.

On Eighth, cutters throw pails of water
on the lawn of flame, and Louis,
holding the canvas hose, hollers:
"No pressure! Nothing coming!"
                        It was close to closing time.

Down on Greene Street, Old Dominick
pushes his wheelbarrow, describes

"a big puff" when windows popped,
glittering showers of glass.
                    It was Spring.

Flaming swords, Pluto piles to Ninth.
Sophie and Della and dozens of others
jump on machine tables; the aisles jammed
with wicker workbaskets and chairs.
                    It was Saturday.

Mrs. Yaller testified: "Some froze at
machines. Others were packed in the cloakroom
filled with smoke. I heard them yelling
in Yiddish or Italian, crying out
the names of their children."
                    It was Payday.

Reporter Bill Shepherd is writing:
"I remember the great strike of last year,
these same girls demanding decent
working conditions."
                    For some it was Sabbath.

Rosie runs to the stairway. The door,
Locked! The telephone, Dead! Piling red
ribbons, fire backs girls into windows.
They stand on sills, see the room
a smashed altar lamp, hear the
screaming novenas of flame.
                    Soon it will be Easter.

Pleats of purple and gold wave,
incandescent filaments of lace snow
in shrapnel of needles and screws.
The blaze from molten bolts stains

glass, walls and lawns—on Cherry Street
sisters nail flowers on tenement doors.
                    It was approaching April.

"I could see them falling,"
said Lena Goldman. "I was sweeping out
front of my cafe. At first we thought
it was bolts of cloth—till they opened
with legs! I still see the day
it rained children. Yes.
                    It was nearly Passover."

Sophie and Della stand on windowsill,
look out on the crazy quilt of town:
*We will leave for our*
*block on Cherry Street,*
*leave these skeletons*
*leaning on machines,*
*the faces fixed on black*
*crucifix of cloakroom window.*
                    It was close to closing time.

The *Times* quotes Mr. Porter: "The Triangle
never had a fire drill—only three factories
in the city have. One man I pleaded
with replied, 'Let em burn. They're
a lot of cattle anyhow.'"
                    It was Spring.

Sophie and Della stand on sill:
*We will leave, our arms*
*around each other, our only*
*sweethearts. Piling red roses*
*two white hearses pull up*
*Cherry Street and the Children*

*of Mary Society march*
*in banners of prayers.*
> It was Saturday.

Captain Henry was the first policeman to arrive:
"I saw dozens of girls hanging from sills.
Others, dresses on fire, leapt from the ledges."
> It was Payday.

Sophie and Della look on crazy quilt of town:
*Fifty of our schoolmates*
*sing in procession:*
*O Trinity of Blessed Light*
*Our Lady of Perpetual Help*
*Ave Maria, Ave Maria*
*Now and at the Hour*
*of the Tarantella.*
> For some it was Sabbath.

Ordering the nets and ladders, Battalion
Chief Worth explains, "I didn't know
they would come down three and even four
together. Why, these little ones went
through life-nets, pavement and all."
> Soon it will be Easter.

Sophie and Della stand on windowsill:
*Look, the flywheel sun sinks*
*in the west. In the Winter*
*Garden, Mr. Jolson springs*
*and bows in blackface.*
> It was approaching April.

*At the Metropolitan Opera*
*George M. Cohan struts "The Rose*
*of Tralee" to the rich trailing*

*in diamond-sackcloth, rending*
*green ashes of dollar bills.*
                    It was nearing Passover.

Sophie and Della stand on sill,
look down crazy quilt of town:
*Intertwined comets we will stream*
*the nightmares of Triangle Bosses*
*Joseph Asch*
*Max Blanck*
*Isaac Harris.*
                    It was close to closing time.

*Our Bosses of the Locked*
*Doors of Sweetheart Contracts*
*who in puffs and tendrils*
*of silent telephones,*
*disconnected hoses, barred*
*shutters, fire escapes*
*dangling in perpetual no*
*help on earth in heaven.*
                    It was Spring.

*The Lord is my shepherd*
*green pastures still*
*waters anointest heads*
*with oil overflowing*
*preparest a table—now*
*our arms around each other*
*we thread the needle where*
*no rich man can go spinning*
*the earth's axle we are*
*leaving in light.*

9

O Lord my God, thou art very great!
Thou art clothed with honor and majesty,
who coverest thyself with
light as with a garment,
who stretchest out the heavens
like a curtain.

—*Psalm 104:1, 2*

# SCRAPS

*Lena Goldman speaks of Sonya*

Garment workers from Triangle always came to my cafe.
Each Saturday the boys and girls in groups, arm in arm
and laughing. You'd think after fourteen hours packing
and sewing they'd be ready to drop! But not on payday.

Sometimes Sonya sat alone, scribbled on scraps.
With such hours at Triangle, five brothers at home,
where else to write? Her poems weren't Moon-June or
like that. At first she only wanted us to laugh.

*There was a cruel boss named Asch*
*who preferred his potatas mashed.*
*When the women talked union, he was thrashin*
*and stewin. Soft-in-the-head, Joseph Asch.*

Oh, she was a bright one! Serious poems too:
*Tonight all over the world*
*garment girls are looking out*
*looking up at stars . . .*

Fourteen years old and writing English!
Well after the Fire, her father came in crying.
"Like losing her twice," he kept saying—
since Sonya's notebook burned up too.

He can't afford to educate his sons.
Yet even in better times, a daughter
wasn't sent to the House of Studies.
"But in America," Sonya said, "I will find my way."

# FOUR FROM SONYA

Is the room swept, blankets
pressed and folded chairs
lined in readiness straight
oh hang the heavenly picture.

Writing poems with a cardboard
bookcase my only company
the poplar tree shifting shades
and whispering: remember me.

Boarding houses yes
lived in four or five or more.
Don't think I'll ever get
the smell of urine, frying
potatas and Evening in Paris
outa my head.

Going outside sunny sunny
rubbing leaves try to
out eclipse each other.

# DEAR UNCLE STANISLAUS

*March 18, 1911*

I pray this letter finds you in good health.
Coming over, a great storm. Water came down the ship
chimneys. Eight drowned. Thanks to Our Lady, I survive.

Uncle, do not believe gold lies in the street.
This is no golden land. Still I have work enough with
bread and meat to eat.

Such noise in this nation! All hours people shout.
Always factory bells and whistles. Up in the loft the
clatter of cloth in machines.

Uncle, write. Tell me, did the potatoes freeze
this Winter? If so, what was to eat? Could you sell
the wheat?

Next to Triangle Waist is a park with flowers and
birds. But who has time to enjoy? Who will pay for
that? Soon it will be Easter and at last a holiday.

They say with everyone coming here, Europe will soon
be empty. Next payday I am sending money. Give my love to
Auntie but save the large part for yourself.

Love,
Marie

P.S. Uncle, did our storks come back this Spring?

# CUTTER AND MOTHER

### 1.

Each morning children squeezed
inside a wire cage that pierced
the pit at extreme speed. *SLAM.*

At six, my mother went to the colliery
alongside her cousins and brothers.
Foremen liked them thin and short

For dynamiting narrow tunnels.
She recalls tall ones were trappers
waiting alone for the rolling-down

Black shaft and only a split-second
to jump aside, open-shut trap door.
She's proud none of her sons spend

Daylight crawling into darkness.
Not harnessed and roped like pit
ponies. No. Not one.


### 2.

Before first shaft of morning
I put bread and cheese in my sleeve,
walk down to Triangle Shirtwaist.

My knife cuts away from daylight,
carves layers round the paper patterns.
Sleeves, collars, flaps; white scraps

Fall to the floor. Pile up dove-tails

wings, eight stories over the streets
and tunnels. But Mother what about

Parts deep inside me, what you can't
see with your eyes. For twelve hours
not a soft word spoken. Machines scream

For more cloth, faster, more cloth.
And at night, to fall exhausted into
dreams that bring no music or painted

Pictures. Mother even the pit pony
that is beaten gets a sweet to eat
pat on her head once in a while.

# IMAGINING THE HORSE

*Captain Meehan's horse, Yale,*
*was the first to arrive on the scene.*

My name is Yale. At first:
Hail of cinders.
Glass. Fire bells.
Falling bales and
timbers. Blood-smell.

Then:
Tarp-covered mounds.
Waterfalls from windows.
Hoses tangled in bundles.
Gutters red to fetlocks.

Night:
Searchlight.
Block and tackle.
Gray men in lines.
Stacks on wagons.

Journey:
Slow pull up Broadway
to Fourteenth to Fourth Avenue to
Twenty-third. Clanging. Wailing.
Twenty-sixth Street Pier.

Dawn:
The Sun has dropped
her mares and foals.
Plentiful as flies.
Wrapped in rows.

# TWENTY-SIXTH STREET PIER

*A temporary morgue*

### 1.

Half-past midnight, a hailstorm
broke, smashing in the roof glass.
Arc lights spun and sputtered,
rain and hail fell on faces in rows.
Policemen swung their lanterns low,
picked out the glass, copied down
numbers from the caskets.

### 2.

I tell ya, folks here still
call the pier "Misery Lane."
Not so long ago you'd see
the blind and insane
beggars and homeless-old
boarding for the poorhouse
or the T.B. hospital.

Boats off to bedlam
or the penitentiary.
Landing them forever
on the islands
in the river.

### 3.

A double line of winos lifted
the bodies, followed the carts
to the Twenty-sixth Street Pier.

Mornings when the families came
panhandlers poured them coffee,
held up the fainting.

You can always get derelicts
to do the dirty work.

4.

*A derelict speaks*

Opium dives, canned-heat alleys
a night in the can's better than
coppers and corpses. I'd rather
the dry-heaves from dogcheap rotgut
or the D.T.s than seeing brothers
search for their sisters or
mothers calling their sons.

# MERCER STREET PRECINCT REPORT

## 1.

One gent's watchcase
one man's garter
one razor strop.

One-half dozen postcards
one yellow metal ring
one one-dollar bill.

One lady's purse with rosary
one small mirror
one pin with painted picture.

## 2.

*One pin with painted picture*

Earthwork windmill rises, arms boxed,
tilts to white heavens. Then little
wood sticks stalk garden walk.

Birds weaving cumulus dive to tulips
named for wishes: Yellow Moonstruck,
Windsor Castle, Tender Shepherd.

Inside shuttered cottage walls,
Kit and Kat lick whiskers, purr
by fire. Kettle spurts water.

# THE FOLLOWING

Sure as smoke follows flame they came:
"Souvenirs from Triangle! Rosaries! Earrings!
Get your machinist's cap—or laces from his boots!
Hair ribbons from a dead girl's head!"

Sure as fish brings flies. Rabbi warned us
"Schnorrers"—solicitors for phony "funeral funds"—
would come when all along it was the Hebrew Free Burial
that was paying. "Sure as flood brings mud," he said.

A few from the Social Register ordered chauffeurs
to drive directly to police lines, demand they
be let through, so as to view this "spectacle."
Sure as carrion brings buzzards.

Ladies in lace shirtwaists, gentlemen in frock-coats
out for a Sunday stroll, filed up Fifth Avenue,
caught the stage-buses to the Twenty-sixth Street Pier.
High-hats in the long lines leading to the dead.

# "I AM APPALLED"

*New York Governor Dix*

The Police Commissioner
points to the Mayor who gripes at
the Governor, "I am appalled,"
who sets on the State Labor Commissioner
who blames the National Fire Underwriters
who turn on the Fire Commissioner
who cites the "City Beautiful"
(for finding fire escapes ugly)
who then faults the Architects
who place it on Tenement Housing
who says failure of the Health Department
who then proclaim conspiracy
between the Utility Companies and
the Police Commissioner.

I made sackcloth also my garment;
and I became a proverb to them.

—*Psalm 69:11*

# AT REST IN GREENWOOD

*Jennie Franco*

My short years wrap me like a cloth
of schooldays, feast days, my First Communion dress.
The cord of mornings, stitching at Triangle
up in the loft before light.

I trace the thread to my last, my fifteenth birthday.
Ribbons of friends dance the Tarantella,
circling plates of tortoni and ices
out on our stoop after dark.

And Mama says, don't forget Our Lady
and always light a holy candle on your birthday.
Today she twists rosary beads between my ruined fingers,
plaits roses in my veil.

Neighbors nail flowers, black crepe
to the doors, they have covered my face
with lilies and forget-me-nots.
I am circled with tapers.

I rest in the front room
next to the room where I was born.
The brass band wraps up our street,
"Panis Angelicus" stops at our stoop.

The Sons of Italy and Saint Angelo Society
have hired a cart just for my flowers.
Papa says, only the best for our Jennie.
A fine lady, I am lifted into my carriage.

The brass-harp of hymns follows the line
of Eleventh Street. Inside its woven voice

I know each murmuring Ave Maria.
The sky smells like lilies.

Slower. Silence. We are nearing Triangle.
Now the shock of the skeleton loft
unfolds the tall wall of wailing till
Heaven cracks and tatters, blesses us with rain.

# FUNERAL FOR THE NAMELESS

*Rose Schneiderman speaks*

For miles the bereaved stream
under a single banner:
"We Demand Fire Protection."

The bunting's blue dye drips down
arms and faces of the honor guard,
eight of our youngest garment girls.

*From the tops of tenements*
*bending out of windows*
*watching us.*

Women, children, the old ones
lean on sashes, stare through
rain screen, down to deep street

Where white horses draped in black net
pull an empty hearse, mountain of blossoms.
*As we march up Fifth Avenue*

*There they are on tops of hundreds of*
*buildings—structures no different from*
*the Asch Building and as for lacking*

*Fire protection, many much worse*
*than Triangle. It is this, not*
*cold rain, that makes me sick.*

At each curb's turning, window-banks
empty of waving white handkerchiefs.
Thunder drums down the narrow stairways.

Thousands pour to Evergreen where over
the empty pits, rabbi, priest, preacher
bless the waiting coffins.

With holy water, hymns, their prayers
pronounce the placards' numerals:
46, 50, 61, 95, 103, 115, 127.

# SURVIVOR'S CENTO

All through the day rain ever and again.
The quartet from the Elks Lodge sang "Abide with Me."
They lost both daughters, Sara and Sarafine.
Last year I was one of the pickets arrested and fined.
We were striking for open doors, better fire escapes.
Freda Velakowski, Ignatzia Bellota, Celia Eisenberg.
You knew the families from the flowers nailed to the doors.
That's my mama. Her name's Julia Rosen.
I know by her hair. I braid it every morning.
Now the same police who clubbed the strikers
keep the crowd from trampling on our bodies.
Sadie Nausbaum, Gussie Bierman, Anna Cohen, Israel Rosen.
I know that's my daughter, Sophie Salemi.
See that darn in her knee? Mended her stockings, yesterday.
Box one-twelve: female, black stockings, black shoes,
part of a skirt, a white petticoat, hair ribbons.
I would be a traitor to these poor burned bodies
if I came to talk good fellowship: Jennie Franco,
Julia Aberstein, Joseph Wilson, Nicolina Nicolese.
I found a mouse on the ninth floor, took it home,
kept it for a pet. At least it was still alive.
Our children go to work in firetraps, come home and sleep
in firetraps. Day and night they are condemned.
Ninth floor looked like a kindergarten. We were eight,
nine, ten. If the Inspector came, they hid us in bins.
Rose Feibush, Clotild Terdanova, Mary Leventhal.
That one's Catherine Maltese, and those, her daughters.
Lucia, she's twenty. Rosalie—she'd be fourteen.
Those two are sisters. Bettina and Frances Miale. M-I-A-L-E.
We asked the Red Cross worker how to help
and she said bring books—Tolstoy, Shakespeare in Yiddish.
Benny Costello said he knew his sister Della by her new shoes.

---

*Cento* is a Latin word for a garment made of patches.

Anna Ardito, Gussie Rosenfield, Sara Kupla, Essie Bernstein,
reminders to spend my life fighting these conditions. Antonia
Colleti, Daisy Lopez Fitze, Surka Brenman, Margaret Schwartz.
One coffin read: Becky Kessler, call for tomorrow.
The eighth casket had neither name nor number. It contained
fragments from the Fire, picked up but never claimed.

# JURY OF PEERS

Morris Baum, sales.
Leo Abraham, real estate.
Abraham Akerstrom, clerk.
Arlington Boyce, management.
H. Houston Hierst, importer.
Harry Roeder, painter.
William Ryan, sales.
Victor Steinman, shirts.
Anton Scheuerman, cigars.
Charles Vetter, buyer.

Mister Hierst summarized:
I've listened to the witnesses
and my conscience is clear.
Harris and Blanck are pretty
good managers. We've reached
the decision that the type
of girl you have at Triangle
is basically less intelligent.
Hell, excuse me, Your Honor,

But most of em can't even read
or speak English—and the way
they live! They're lots
less intelligent than the
type of female you find
in other walks of life. I mean
that kinda worker is more—
well—susceptible to panic.
Emotional females can't

Keep a clear head they
panicked and jumped my

41

conscience is clearly
Act of Almighty
God they jumped
conclusion Your
Honor owners
of Triangle
not guilty.

The children which thou shalt have
after thou has lost the others
shall say again in thy ears:
The place is too strait for me;
give place to me that
I may dwell.
—*Isaiah 49:20*

# GRAND STREET

*After Sophie Ruskay*

We lined the walks in chalk boxes, numbers.
Played potsy with markers of tin. Or spinning
tops, we'd only stop for the hokeypokey man who
sold a slap of ice cream on a piece of paper for
a penny. Papa complained potsy and dancing wore
shoe soles through in just two weeks and told us
not to leave our block. Still I skipped to

Grand Street to dream at the dolls in windows.
Each splendid in real silk and lace. Blue eyes,
golden hair. Their brass-bound trunks for travel
brimmed kidskin boots and fur-trimmed bonnets.
One Mamselle in ashes-of-roses held a pink parasol.
At her feet, a white batiste shirtwaist was displayed.
The kind Mama made at Triangle. Back before the Fire.

# WHITE LIGHT

*After Sonya Levien*

It's not easy to teach us union.
Garment girls shift like sand, start
too young in the trade, wait for

Prince Charming to take em away.
When I arrived from Russia
my cheeks like apples. And look now!

But talk about a dreaming fool!
Me, thirteen in the Golden Land
longing to work at Life and Love.

Be what you call a builder of bridges.
I'd go back, show all Moscow
a great American lady.

My first position: feeding kerchiefs
to machine. First English sentence:
"Watch your needle—three thousand stitches

A minute." I was some swift kid in
those days: seventy-two hundred
an hour, eighty-six thousand pieces

A day, four dollars in the pay
envelope—and that the busy season.
For three months my pay was bread.

I yearned to earn wages, save my
little sister's passage, I was so
lonely in America. Soon like the rest

I grieved at my machine, swore I'd
marry any old man just to get out.
One by one the others left to marry

But returned to Triangle. I saw
my future in a white heat light
no dreams could soften.

# SHIRTWAIST TUCKER

*Sadie Hershy*

The Fire? That was
Nineteen-and-eleven.
Yes I was a garment girl
a tucker at Triangle.
We'd haul big bolts of cloth
feed em to pleating machines
that crimped the folds
at neck and wrists—
to take in fullness or
decorate the yoke.
Saturday was payday—
twelve dollars for sixty hours!
Oh I could make do
better than most though.
Winter was bitter
and prices dear.
Bit by bit bought me
a warm wool coat.
And in Spring
a white batiste waist.
Was a real American lady
come High Holy Days!
Say that was a slave-driving place.
Couldn't talk to your neighbors
and the bosses kept doors locked.
Looking out for organizers.
Agitators.
That afternoon I was close by
the cutting-table
spied a little snake of smoke.
So I says to the manager

"Mr. Bernstein I see smoke."
And when he tipped water from
a little wooden bucket
such a flame shot up!

# POTTER'S FIELD

*Thomas Horton speaks.*

A few of us back then were porters in the district
bundling scraps under the cutting-table or
after the packers crated the shirtwaists—why,
we'd haul them on down to Washington Place.
My grammaw told me when she was a girl
Washington Park was a potter's field and used
to say the nameless passed to glory anyway.
Soon as the high-class built here, potter's field
became a park with bushes and benches,
a garden spot for their fancy townhouses.
(We laughed at how those homeless bones
were pushing up a monument to President Washington
who once sold a slave for a bolt of cotton cloth.)
Then the factories came and company housing—
tenements you call em. Crowded! You don't know
the word! But you want to hear about the Fire.

Well, Giuseppe had fainted so I ran the car with Gaspar.
When the fire broke out and the elevator broke down
I kept the machine from smashing in the basement.
'Cause of the smoke we couldn't see the floors
had to open up the doors by guesswork.
Girl, I ran that car till it couldn't run
why we were puttin in switch cables
till they ran with water and stuck.
Circuit breakers were blowing out all over the place.
The ladies were jumping on my car, even slid down
the ropes—why there were twenty on the roof!
The ones that got inside grabbed at Gaspar's arms,
pulled his hair, jabbed his face. Christ A-mighty!
They were climbin on the cables!

That was the passenger car, you understand.
Later I read in the *Tribune* a big iron bar locked
the freight elevators—no, never could use em.
I'm the only Negro to testify at the trial.
The headlines named me "Heroic Elevator Man."

# STITCHER

*For Judith Hall*

It was soon after the Fire
I was employed as a housemaid.
Now I wash the garments and
some I starch. Stiff as grief

Or courage. The flat iron presses
and gives shine. In the morning
there are lamps to fill, globes
wiped so light can shine through.

Windows thrown open for sweeping
and dusting. Mid-days, Mistress
sometimes recites scriptures or
legends like Paramhansa the swan

Who could sup up milk, leave
water in the saucer. She says we
separate pure from impure in our
breathing, that new cells replace

The old. I know remade garments
bring fair material from that
judged hopeless and so my needle
joins torn places, mends worn parts.

Each stitch carries a blessing.
Don't you know handkerchiefs keep
secrets, that hat trims see hair
as a halo of the spirit, crown of

Life? A skillful housemaid will not
pour boiling water over flannel or

use strong soap on silk or organdy.
I've learned the language in the

Evenings. Alphabet. Vocabulary.
Grammar rote by gaslight sputter.
Tonight I write this history into
my copy book: Gehenna. Gehenna,

A word for garbage burning outside
the walls of Jerusalem. The refuse
of the city. Corpses of criminals.
Sacrificed animals. Holocausts of

Relics, regrets, evil memories
released into smoke.

# SACRISTAN

That first winter after the Fire I came
to our convent. My assignment is to tidy
the sacristy and sanctuary. Before Mass,
I take the silver from closet, fill cruets
with wine and water; place pressed linen
under pallboard, over chalice, lavabo bowl.

The priest's vestments must be laid out
just so. Blue for Lady Day, purple for Lent,
white for first-class feasts, green for
ordinary. Always red to commemorate death-
dates of martyrs. We study the lives of
Lawrence and Saint Joan and in the symbol

Book, look up their signs of stake and
gridiron. When the sanctuary lamp burns
low, I'll trim the wick and fill it with
oil. Trade candelabra stubs for tall
taking care to pare beeswax drips from tops
of golden holders. Fresh charcoal, sandalwood

Incense for the censor. And now to work
before the morning bell! Rags, brushes,
mops. Scrub and shine the steps, pews,
floor. Ora labora. Labora Ora. Prayer is
labor. Labor is prayer. I polish and pray
the names of my brother and the other shirtwaist

Martyrs so these holy ones may intercede for
us on earth. In my monastic breviary, I mark
any mention of fire or garments and collect
those psalms into a copy book. I've composed
a homily on the example of the beekeeper
who handles her charges yet is not stung.

# NINTH FLOOR REPRISE

*Fifty-eight girls crowded into a cloakroom.*

The glass blackens and shatters.
Who will come for us?

Up on Tenth, typists and bookkeepers leave
ledgers to ashes, machines to melt.
The packers and switchboard-lady gone
the phone cords and crate slats spurt
split into stars and meteors.

Up on Tenth, our finished shirtwaists unfold,
crack the crates, jump upright, join sleeves,
dance the hora and mazurka, spin like dreidels.
They call to us, their makers:
Stitcher, Presser, Cutter, Tucker.

"I saw them piled," testified Fireman Wohl,
"they pressed their faces toward a little window."

Gather up the fragments that
remain, that nothing be lost.
—*John 6:12*

# STADIUM SESTINA

*Remembering high school commencement
while researching the Triangle Fire of March 25, 1911.*

The poorest student—me—with the loudest voice reads the script:
"Mother of Exiles from her beacon-hand. . . ."
Our town in the stadium bleachers looks down on circumstance.
In the east, the Triangle papers slowly rise on imperfect wings
of file folders, pamphlets, fly to this valley of newsprint
song sheets. Where are the words of fire for my generation?

Our parents and teachers became the first generation
after that of 1911, the year these martyrs taught History the script.
Their shredded alphabets of flames pierced the clouds of newsprint.
(Ashes are drifting seventy years to light on my left-writer's hand.)
At Commencement, our graduation sleeves split in wings.
The orchestra strikes up Pomp and Circumstance.

The owners of Triangle profited from fires (all were created
circumstance).
From Europe, Italy, Jamaica, Palestine, Russia—the immigrant
generation
crossed to Ellis Island, bundles piled, shawls spread in wings.
Each wage-earner signed an "X" or Arabic-Cyrillic-Hebrew script.
On payday, March 25, 1911, no one knew how many were on hand—
the hired and fired, dispensable as newsprint.

The *Herald*, *Sun*, *Telegraph*, and *Times* set photos into newsprint,
hurried to interview witnesses, each tried to scoop the circumstance.
. . . Now Commencement ends. The principal shakes my hand,
pronounces: "We pass the torch to a new generation."
Every year the same old line ends the script.
Whether graduation or when our town's a tour-stop for the Wings

Over Jordan Choir—black angels singing God's chillen got
shoes / harps / wings.

Since the time of Triangle, turpentine torches of rags and newsprint
were replaced by gas lamps, then by electric arc lights. So says
    the *Script*
*for the Centennial.* Citizens in beards and bonnets recreated the
    circumstance
and Miss Liberty raised her beacon flashlight beside golden
    generations
of post-Depression years. (Few thought McCarthyism had gotten
    out of hand.)

The pageant showed the founding of our town and how folks lived
    hand-to-hand
until Henry Ford and the Great War opened Prosperity's
    war-bond-wings
over Union Carbide and the First National Bank. But the pilgrim
    generation
inside Triangle bent their backs, stitched at flimsy thinner than
    newsprint.
The scrap piles, oil pans, and wicker baskets their circumstance.
Families followed the multiple hearses. One father held a
    pasteboard script

In his hand: "This is the funeral of Yetta Goldstein." He follows
    the newsprint
march-map under clouds split in wings. "Heavens Wept" headlines
    the circumstance.
All this before Commencement or my generation—back when flames
    wrote in script.

# TRIANGLE SITE

*Asch Building, 1911; Brown Building, 1981*

Soaked to skin, look through lens
at Eighth, Ninth, Tenth. So this
is where they worked, I thought

How hot the loft on summer days
and say aloud the layers learned
from photogravure fashion plates:

Pantaloons, petticoats, hour-glass
corsets, one cover called a camisole.
So many strings! In the spinning

Mills down South, steam looms boomed
and even in Winter children stripped
to their shifts, baby hands slick

On cotton bobbins. The shutter clicks,
a pigeon struts and springs. So this
is where they fell. Or jumped.

Layers billow, catch broken rails,
like sails slap on light posts or
pile high on iron fence spears

Where like a little boat, one
pierced shoe holds a paper rose
stem up.

# SEAR

*July 1982*

Always adding. Revising this manuscript.
I plant *direct quotations* on the page,
arranging line-breaks, versification.

Newspaper files: Frances Perkins speaks
from the street, *I felt I must sear it
not only on my mind but on my heart
forever.* One mother, *When will it be
safe to earn our bread?* Their words.
Yet some call that schmaltz, soap-opera-

*Sentiment, Victorian melodrama.* Riding
the subway, smoke fizzes in my ears and
in my room, electric heater coils glow
Cs and Os in the box. To write about *them*
yet not interfere, although I'm told
a poet's task is to create a little world.

A testimony: Two tried to stay together
on the ledge, but one suddenly twisted
and plunged, a burning bundle. The other
looked ahead, arms straight out, speaking
and shouting *as if addressing an invisible
audience.* She gestured an embrace then

Jumped. Her name was Celia
Weintraub. She lived
on Henry Street.

# THE DAY WHEN MOUNTAINS MOVED

The mountain-moving day is coming.
I say so, yet others doubt.
Only awhile a mountain sleeps.
In the past
All mountains moved in fire
Yet you may not believe it.
Oh man, this alone believe
All sleeping women now will
awake and move.
*—Yosano Akiko, 1911*

# SOURCES

Elson, Hilbert. "Improved Labor Laws Result from Triangle Fire Fifty Years Ago." *Industrial Bulletin* (Albany, N.Y.), March 1961.

Howe, Irving, and Kenneth Libo. *How We Lived: A Documentary History of Jews in America 1880–1930*. Richard Marek Publishers, Inc., New York, 1979.

Kuniczak, W. S. *My Name Is Million: An Illustrated History of the Poles in America*. Doubleday & Company, Inc., New York, 1978.

Militz, Annie. *Spiritual Housekeeping*. Master-Mind Press, Los Angeles, 1925.

O'Sullivan, Judith, and Rosemary Gallick. *Workers and Allies: Female Participation in the American Trade Union Movement 1824–1976*. Smithsonian Institution Press, Washington, D.C., 1975.

Saperstein, Saundra. "Reliving Pain." *The Washington Post*, February 1, 1979.

Schneiderman, Rose, and Lucy Goldwaithe. "Triangle Memorial Service." In *All for One*. Paul S. Ericksson, Inc., Middlebury, Vt., 1967.

Stein, Leon, ed. *Out of the Sweatshop*. Fitzhenry and Whiteside, Ltd., Toronto, 1977.

Stein, Leon. *The Triangle Fire*. J. B. Lippincott Company, Philadelphia, 1962.

Wertheimer, Barbara. *We Were There*. Pantheon Books, New York, 1977.

## *Illustrations*

1. HESTER STREET
   Courtesy of the Library of Congress
2. SIDEWALK DEAD
   Courtesy of Brown Brothers
3. TRADE UNION PROCESSION FOR FIRE VICTIMS
   Courtesy of the Library of Congress
4. SHIRTWAIST STRIKERS
   Courtesy of the Library of Congress
5. GARMENT GIRLS, *June 1911*
   Courtesy of Mrs. Florence Leebov, Pittsburgh
6. JEWISH CUSTOMS ON THE BROOKLYN BRIDGE
   Courtesy of the Library of Congress
7. LIPSHITZ & EISENBERG
   Courtesy of the Library of Congress